The Gatherer

12/7/14

The Gatherer

Poems by Judith Bowles

Turning Point

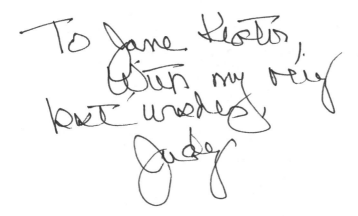

Published by Turning Point
P.O. Box 541106
Cincinnati, OH 45254-1106

ISBN: 9781625491046
LCCN: 2014950786

Poetry Editor: Kevin Walzer
Business Editor: Lori Jareo

Visit us on the web at www.turningpointbooks.com

Cover art:
Museo Thyssen-Bornemisza / Scala / Art Resource, NY
Hotel Room. 1931. Oil on canvas, 152.4 x 165.7 cm. Dimension
with frame: 168 x 182 x 10 cm. Inv. N.: 1977110.
Hopper, Edward (1882-1967)
Museo Thyssen-Bornemisza, Madrid, Spain

Acknowledgments

My gratitude is extended to the following journals:

Innisfree Journal of Poetry: "The Fisherman," "Joyful Noise"

Delmarva Review: "The Instrument," "My Parkinson's and I Attend My 30th Reunion"

Gargoyle: "L.S.M.F.T."

This book remembers my parents Grace and Harry LeFever, my brother Joe. I am thankful for the careful, steadfast attention of the Surrey Street Poets and of our teacher David Keplinger, who lights the dark path and shows us the way home.

Table of Contents

III. The Gatherer

For Tom

And for our daughters, Julia, Amy, and Lauren

The paths to the house I seek to make
But leave to those to come the house itself.

Walt Whitman

I.

How to Get from My Mother's House
to Mine

After Hopper's *The Hotel Room*

A woman like a swimmer
at the edge of a pool
turns her back to the glare
looks toward a book,
heavy on her knees,
loose in her hands.
Her face so in shade
that only the angle
of her chin and the angle
of the book indicate
something besides its words
are on her mind.
She is nearly naked,
her full smooth legs
another kind of glow
against the white
anchored sheet.
A creamy pink chemise
wraps her torso
like another skin.
Why does it seem
something is going to happen
or has happened here?
Her dress lying draped
across the heavy armchair,
two pieces of luggage
standing closed and tagged,
black pumps askew
on the carpet, deep green
like the chair
and the wall to the left.
A perfect kind of balance

is at play here, the dislocation
in an order of its own.
So much has gathered
in this room where colors
have their own sense of play
and relief, next to
a wide window
noisy with light.

How to Get from My Mother's House to Mine

Leave when you are very young before language
entangles your urge toward light
and leave early in the morning before coffee blooms
in the kitchen with its promise of warmth.
Take the numbers in your street address
write them the early way
you understood them:
twenty, then ninety then two.
Also your phone number: KIngswood 2481
while we're talking of magic.
Let your red Schwinn bike carry you past
city houses to small flat farms and barns
where your pony will snort when she sees you
ready to trot to the cinder path that traces
the Scioto River beyond the outburst
of a dam to the grave of Chief Leatherlips
where his Wyandot name, *Same Size as Blue,*
was the first poem you learned.

But this is all local stuff. You'll need to go further
and a compass will help you head south
and then north in the tumult of years up ahead.
This is, after all, more than a day's journey
we are talking of here and much of it
will be undertaken at night while you sleep.
The searching for pocketbooks, children, doctors,
the loss of birds, wallets, fathers,
brothers, many of whom become stones
is serious and ceaseless work and it must be done
with precision. This is how houses are made

and mine is no different. If you've done the labor
I'm easy to find.

St. Mary's of the Springs

The circle my boot made in the slush-melt of snow
was a way to show Sister that I had no answer

and that fear of her hell and her God
was nothing compared to the fear of what lay

consecrated under her starched blazing wimple
pressing her cheeks into balloons of pale flesh

quivering with the question she repeated like a rosary
her hands circling, one around the other

in the heavy cuffed sleeve of her pitchy habit.
An orbit that itself was perpetual hell.

Obdurate
I learned how to be under her gaze and only now

can offer the coveted forgiveness to myself,
that non-Catholic girl who took something

that was not my own because
I could not live without that sugar-laden

egg, embroidered as it was with luscious
pink rosettes and shining within, a family

of tiny bunnies dancing. I didn't win
the race that would have won the egg

but gave myself permission to take it nonetheless.
It was, despite the weather, Easter

and I had planned, in my unstingable soul
to carry it home to my mother.

Aftermath

At age eleven my numbers froze
and refused arrangement

as in the addsubtractmultiplydivide
fifth grade workbook and my dry

tongue caught flame that swept
away memory from the roof of my mouth.

It was spring; I didn't care.
I stopped doing math and rode my horse.

She was frisky after winter, wanted to gallop.
I let her, to her heart's content, until her sweat

sprayed like suds into my eyes and it was over.
My father had carried a suit from the guest

closet into his bedroom and put it on.
The fabric was dense,

the buttons cold against my cheek.
Out the screen door the cigarette he flipped

made a high-flying arc into the shrub.
He went off to the Navy like he was going to work

at his office. My mother, distracted
sat on my bed every night doing times tables

with me. Her hands were full
with an ashtray, a cigarette, my math book.

She passed along numbers like stones.
I took them, placed them where they belonged.

We built a wall of the things I couldn't forget.
It was the hardest job Mother and I ever had.

Elegy for Opal Harper

Our big stone home was a hollow
where silence muffled the walls.
Sitting two steps up from the bottom
of the stairs I gave into its weight
and sobbed into the crook of my arm.
The new maid came from the kitchen,
sat next to me, put my hand in hers,
the color of caramel cream, and waited
with me on the second step up
until I looked at her, at Opal Harper,
and was able to smile. It made
her so happy that I started to laugh
and hugged her before I knew even
her name.
Have you ever looked at an opal?
The stone is warm, smooth,
and like milk with a rainbow swirl
that shimmies just under its surface.

Slough

We told our mothers
that the mud sucked us in
and we meant it.

Rain had lifted.
As if snapped back
into low-hanging clouds
it left earth dark
and foggy soft
oozing under our feet
between our toes
on the dirt road.
Earth gave up its crust.

It showed us some secrets
in watery form we could touch.
Without thought we reached

into its heart with our toes
and learned how it felt
to go slack like the mud

to smear our skin
with its sludge,
paint each other with stockings

up to our knees
and then higher.
We talked of our mothers'

long gloves wiping our arms
to the armpits

then chocolate cheeks
and with wide
open mouths
a taste on the tongue.

Mud sucked us in
to someplace we knew
in our bodies
slipping under our fingers.
We abandoned all stories
for this one.

The Architect

This man with the rolled sleeves
sits at his wide desk under a wide window,
looks into the light like a farmer
scanning the field he just plowed.

Edward Hopper's people
never look as if they're being watched.
They are saturated with their own lives.
He painted them in the midst.

This man is entirely absorbed by the city
and the light. The sun's
to his right; long shadows fall
left. He becomes what he sees,

even the sky slabbed over everything
is smeared on his shirt. The blue is all there.

For John Millington Synge

I was in plays during college
one after the other.
Our prompter was someone in crew
who had already done lights
and had time, with the script
in her lap, to fill in the silence
of a missed cue or lapse in mid-stream.

The crumbs eaten by birds
came back *sotto voce* intact:
...or the poets of the Dingle Bay

and I've heard all times it's the poets
are your like, fine fiery fellows
with great rages when their temper's roused.

My lines in her mouth
traced by her finger
on their Irish road

that had emptied themselves
into space before I could find
a way to make them my own

still had their magic
to bring me awake
like a song

I'd been waiting to sing.
There was nothing flat from Ohio
in the cadence. I wanted those words
in my mouth to save me.

Shadow

I love this self
released
into what rides
ahead or behind me

as light
interrupted
that slides
along sidewalks

and refers
to me
in outline only

way beyond
any substance
I could summon.

*

At the intersection, wide and open
where the library faces
the Catholic Church my shadow
slips off the curb
while I wait for the car to turn
and remember not just Ted Hughes' name
but the hard bloody kiss
he gave Sylvia Plath in the kitchen
when they first met.

*

Nobody seems to be fond
of Prince Charles except me.
I've seen his mind as laid
out in plots at Highgrove
the garden that shows
what he loves,
this son of a queen
who placed an enamel portrait
of his grandmum in the center
of plywood sun rays where
she watches him still,
and a small ochre temple
set in the shade
to honor Ted Hughes
his loved, laureled friend.

*

When my spade hit the stone
it urged me out of its way
as it groped for an opening
tenderly, seeking softness
almost sniffing its way
to a purchase
as though darkness
were its element
and its assignment was to seek
a footing without even knowing.
Everything has an edge.

The Wind is a Generous Donor

Ants thrive on the seeds of adder's tongue,
sun spurge, and bindweed but betony gives them
a sweet dreamless sleep. Their aching antennae
discover wallflower, furze, fat-hen
before fever-few gives spasm a rest.

Love-lies-a-bleeding and statice fill
this three-jointed hour-glass
with sufficient delight whether chewing
or lugging their fresh-from-the-field finds.
Penny-cress spills her gifts, a windfall
that shames even blue pimpernel or mugwort's
posterity.

A full-armored army of soldiers at the ready,
passing the treasure in a bucket brigade today
and tomorrow sow-thistle's their target,
ripe and rich, their own vein of gold.
Wild carrot, wild oats and wild leek
are on their spring menu, filling
both soil and thorax
with burgeoning goods.

A Joyful Noise

The comfrey's bell-shaped flowers
are wobbling with bees in busy
birth-like clusters this morning.
Life after life nuzzles in and out of dainty snouts
that seem an endless source of sustenance
for the yellow-dusted carriers.

Last fall they swooned in shock, lay down
their dark lance leaves and all but said farewell
after the transplanting. Cadaverous they lay
and I took them at their desiccated word
as goners. Now they're running April riot
like an army at the border

who've summoned a fleet of buzzing
allies to spread the loot once ravaged.

Parsley Sweetens the Air

All I can think of this morning is parsley
and the hungry birds in my garden taking
seed from what's left of the iris and salvia
both blue in their day, that spilled
from the slippery weight of the bag
held askew toward the feeder
spilled back to the ground in a heap
onto sear leaf, now both a match for color
one burdened under the other
until black-bibbed sparrows, single file
as if on a dare, dart out from the holly
for a beakful, tear toward what's left
of wisteria to balance and swallow
the firm millet ovule reborn in a song
rising sweet-swéet, sweet-swéet.

Softness of Pollen

My lily changes light into food—
an alchemist with a swarm of recipes
to stir up the senses of the least
busy bee in the neighborhood
who is lost in a summer daze
and forgotten the softness of pollen
dusting his thighs
like a man lounging on Sunday
an escapee of time.

II.

My Mother's Music

My Mother's Music

Mullion was a terrible word, she said
that sounded nothing like what it signified:
straight measured lines on glass each fit
snugly into a base and in its slight span,
interrupted light—
Mother ate tomato and mayonnaise sandwiches
at the breakfast table, squirting red and white juice
onto *National Geographic*'s shiny pages
and showed me pictures of the jewel
squid who lives a transparent life
a thousand lung-crushing feet
under the Atlantic Ocean.
One of its mismatched eyes was larger
than the other to scope for prey in the deep's
darkness. That, she said, is what *mullion*
sounds like.

Rather than stories at night sometimes
my brother and I asked for her old-fashioned
sad songs so we could hear the hollow
mourning in her voice. She smoothed
her pompadour as if the words might blow
it astray as she sang of a girl who died
before her father got home from war;
a Mother who coughed away her life
while her son clung to her chest
and always, always, *Frankie and Johnny*.
We wept and learned of some strange
joy in our tears and thrilled thinking
of Frankie pulling back her kimono
(nearly naked beneath) for her small .44
where, every night in our house on Essex Road

Johnny got what was coming to him.
Mother crossed her arms over her chest
and hung on to every vowel like candy
too good to swallow.
Well roll me over on my left side boys
Roll me over so slow.

Flash-Frozen

My mother grew up in a homemade world.
Her mother stitched sunbonnets
one stitch at a time for five little girls,
carried pears, beans, tomato, squash
in her apron from the garden to the kitchen
where steaming mason jars with wide
open mouths stood at the ready
to receive. Jars lined the cool
basement shelves like picture books
wild with color, waiting for another
season. A huge grey pot, quiet
on the stove made soup for the week.
In winter, root vegetables bounced,
softened in water fragrant with the earth.

Clarence Birdseye, born in Brooklyn,
practiced taxidermy before joining
the Department of Agriculture
as a naturalist posted in the Arctic.
There he learned a thing or two
watching the Inuit make holes in the ice
drop lines and bring up a fish, frozen
straight through in the blink of an eye.
Clarence brought that thought home
in a system that packed food
into waxed-cardboard cartons,
flash-frozen, nearly fresh.
My mother's freezer was as big as a car.
Thursdays were poker night.
She could whip up a meal in twenty minutes
once she unwrapped the box.

Second Sight

My grandmother's blind eyes look
everywhere at once in memory of sight
and follow sound as though it were her light.

My footsteps tell her I am coming down the hall.
My name is called before I turn into her room
where her dark rocker sits angled at the window

toward the light and toward the door.

Her papery hands are agents toward
but not against the dark which she has entered
like a book that had been assigned. Her words

ring clear as they have always done, and she leans
into them as though to deepen the engraving,
hands circling as if clearing windows as she speaks.

*Remember I've told you about the terrible day when
I was five and went with Mama to the well? How
she was seized with such a fit and died while I stood
and watched and held the bucket?*

Now her memory grips a handle and her voice a
secret hush.

*I never told a soul one other thing, how she lay still
and wet herself. I poured water there as if it spilled.*

Early Death

The water in the well held deep and cold
after the snowmelt, as if it had come from the sky
and not from the rocky heart of the earth.

Mother fastened my black rubber boots
and at each click I laughed as she winked.
I blew brilliant circles into rainbows

that shimmied on the frosted glass
then took my warm breath
into puffs all the way to the well.

So much shone that morning, light
held us up to see ordinary things
in their perfect arrangement. I thought

it was an animal coming from the
woods that caused Mother to start,
but something else seized her, was shaking

her, taking her, that made every sound stop,
even breathing.
The rope had to be creaking, the birds

if not singing, must have been rustling
the leaves, but not to my ears
which closed on that morning.

Later I remembered the moss,
moist between stones, weeping and furry.
The heavy oak bucket rocking on its rope
emptied of water, pitchy black.

The Instrument

The piano took up the corner
in our living room
like a fat girl
at a party
who nobody talked to.

Morning light sloped toward it
from an east window,
and later,
the west one
lightened and tried.

Nothing could pound it to life.
Not my brother's
wide flat hands,
or the shudder
when he slammed the lid.

It was our babysitter's husband
waiting for his wife
in the dark room
who played "Harbor Lights"
and I knew the words.

What I heard
from under his fingers
hovered and shook
(he was a war vet)
all over the keys.

The music he played
was not separate

from sorrow.
Sorrow could be heard
as a song.

Playing with Fire

My brother kept the Ohio matches in his top desk drawer.
He leaned his elbows on both sides of his book
rested his fists on his chin and into his cheeks
and chewed on a match while he read.
I wondered if he'd noticed that Grandfather Errett
swished his cigar back and forth in his mouth
spitting and chewing it down to a nub.
The matches felt like the balsa wood of his
unfinished model planes that lay as if broken
on the floor in front of his bookcase.
Their boxes were scattered around his room
rattling with brushes, stick-on insignias and
official colors of shiny paint.

One day he told me that all of his planes were crippled
and had to be burned. I started to tell him that they
could be fixed, that maybe someone could help
but his mind was made up. I imagined painting them
into the Mustangs and Spitfires they might have been.
He held each one, there must have been six or seven,
over the waste paper basket and whispered a *pow*
as it dropped. I thought about all that paint going
   to waste.

He told me they made the matchsticks square
to be easy to hold and they were. We'd carried
the basket to the wilderness side behind our house,
where the driveway ended by the stone wall
where he went to break bottles against the trashcan.
When glass smashed against drum
our dog ran in circles and howled
until the bottles as bottles were gone.

He clicked lighter fluid round and round
over the planes, saying they had to be
drowned before they were burned.
Grandfather Errett claimed he could spit
on a fire and stop it but the flames rising
out of that basket that day were fueled with more
than one man could contain. Then my brother said
watch and he clicked out our names on the driveway,
gave me the square match to light the gigantic
J's. Our names were in flame.

Even High in the Green Apple Tree

I dropped to the ground like a stone when you called me
and ran to the kitchen door you held open with your foot
so you could keep reading the book in your hands
and not notice how in my scrambling to get there
I fell up the stone steps and skinned one hand, one knee

and was glad that you hadn't seen me be clumsy
because you would have laughed and that laugh
was worse than the blood on my hand or my knee
and mainly I was in a hurry to catch you before
          you changed
your mind about being with me which could happen
in a flash

                    but today you were waiting
and I followed you through the kitchen up
          the carpeted steps around
the landing into your room like a well-trained
          little sister who studied
everything you did and memorized you in a million
          ways how you laid
"Beautiful Joe" on the desk with both hands
          then motioned
with your left for me to sit and I slid down to the rug
          with my back

to the radiator and watched your face as you
leaned to the radio and switched on the worn
          wooden knob
while shushing me sternly as if I were talking—
then for a moment there was silence except for our
breath until an announcer with a voice like a man

calling through a long tunnel said,
"From out of the west with the speed of light..."
and galloping music and hooves took me out
of your room.

Reese Witherspoon is Happy at Last

The saddest thing in the world is a beautiful person
who's miserable in marriage, has two darling children
and has to get out and away from the mess.
Doesn't that just make you sick no matter how
        much money
and beauty they have if they can't find their ray
        of sunshine?
Well, this story has a Hollywood ending that *People*
calls "Reese's Perfect Day!"
If that doesn't give you goose bumps, just read
        "in a laid-back,
at-home wedding mixing classic elegance with
        country chic,
a joyful Reese says 'I do' to Jim Toth."
That pretty much says it all right there.
You can read the article about her rustic ranch in some
valley, how she let her kids be the scene stealers in their
darling clothes, how she wore her signature blonde hair
straight and simple, carried those big English roses,
walked down the aisle to "Keep on the Sunny
        Side of Life"
for heaven's sake, and got her diamond wedding
        band under
an arbor of flowers. Everyone went wild
        and cheered like
a baseball game. Afterward was a sunset cocktail party
where the drinks had juice from her ranch.
Reese's own parents were there to give the wedding
a real family feel. There were menus showing two
        mules neck
in neck with an R and J underneath. The meal was farm
inspired since Reese keeps horses, goats, pigs and

50

chickens and everything's down-to-earth.
They made chandeliers out of wood and mason jars
all lit with candles. Who ever came up with that I wonder?
And the guests, you'd have thought you were at the
Academy Awards or Miss America. Everyone under
that big Hollywood sun was there. Even Renee Zellweger
who many confuse with Reese, because of their names, but
not on that night, not by a long shot. My brother says
Reese has everything going for her except a fixed income
but some people can't take other people's happiness.

Noises Off

How can light
arrive without
sound? Think
of the glittering
motion, the rigorous
luminous quiver
that manages
to glide and sweep
into the eye
before it can blink.
That beam
rakes through
and displaces dark
in an ambush
complete.
It simply ignites
what should
in molecular terms
be a noisy event.

My Parkinson's and I Attend My 30th Reunion

How can I go as myself without him
my Parkinson's? For one night, these
few hours, to be shed of his weight—
a huge hand on my chest daring me forward
alone, now he's stopped my gallop.

How can I go as myself without him
whose fingers telegraph such urgent
signals in a language out of history
that my body receives as punctuation
points. A word is a jolt
and has made me his meme.

How can I go as myself without him
when he's watched in the wings so long
to claim me from everything I was about:
a black bike, a pea-green diving board,
low hurdles, white lines on a cinder track.
Now we're twinned in a three-legged race
to the close. I'm ahead of my classmates.

How can I go as myself without him
who holds the baton and is leading
my life on the metrical path
that his name has laid down.
I am blind to its turnings
and have no other guide.

Measure for Measure

Let the morning be quiet
the cool air message be everything
except the dew settled
silent and brief.

May there be nothing unhushed
except breathing, its soft percussion
and the song of a speechless heart
which gives and receives in measure
so utterly equal, its action
replenishes itself.

Abandon all stories for this one.

Put your hand on your chest
or your throat or your wrist
feel the rich coursing motion
that proves air made liquid
becomes air again.

My House Cricket
(Acheta domesticus)

This morning the cricket is dead in my basement
like dozens before him, no, dozens of dozens.
Their lives are measured in months
and they are old when they come in from the cold.
I thought my cat did them in but he's gone
and they keep up with the dying.

Last night the cricket leapt high in the air
when I came down the stairs and I stopped,
so did he, and he chirped, two or three strums
of his scraper along the teeth of a file
under his wing. A mating call
which the female hears with ears
in her knees. Think of it!
She has a receiving station
in the joint of a limb
that can maneuver toward
or away from love or danger.

When I came down the stairs I stopped.
So did he, except for two wavering antennae
casting in air like long fishing lines
that seemed to be reaching toward me.

Mr. Cavins' Chemistry

He gave us questions and I watched
the burner's blue flame lick the smooth test tube
into bubbles. They wavered in the water like the frogs'
eggs I studied in a lab next door.
The male we learned, wraps himself
around the female from behind.

He might hold her in his grip like that with special
thumb pads which, miraculously, rise up in season
then like a dream are gone. He might hold her there
like that for several days. A kind of sexual rigor mortis
come to life because the holding

tells her eggs to start their journey
through the oviducts and out of her body, each
with a jelly coat, to lay and wait to be completed.
My test tube showed eggs swell up, rise up
unending numbers Mr. Cavins said,
while there was flame, water and a container.

III.

The Gatherer

Edison's Petition

The chair is sturdy, must be oak.
The slatted back is taller
than any man or woman's head.
The arms curl round to rest the hands.
Were it not bolted to the floor
it could sit easily in the reading room
of your library down the street.
The room it sits in has a clock,
a window looking out to chairs
looking in, a lever made of bronze
beside the second door, and on the wall
beside a shelf, a telephone.
One hanging light is overhead.
When lit it casts no shadow
and shows the straps now open wide
like a man's unbuckled belt, waiting.

Look into Light

Tell me why when I stand
upstairs and see a tiny slip of light
between the floorboards my mind lifts
its head? Something deeper than breath

opens my breath as I look into light
that is way out of reach but carries
huge weight and a memory of space
before wood took its place. This cottage,

now mine, was built by a man for his daughter.
He carried it home in his head as a wish
from the Cotswolds and made it come true.
It was not always here. The stones

and lumber, windows and doors,
not always here. Erase this place
then me, my family before and now.
What remains is not memory, but space.

The Selkie's Peedie Lass
Seal people of Orkney legend

I am of the sea and always was safe
in the currents that carried
my body though *body*
and its word were beyond
the brightness that held me.

I was swept into a wave
that rushed overhead
like a dazzle of dusk before dark
and raised to the warmth
of rocks littering
Orkadian shores.

I settled my treasure of self
in the sun. Shed of my skin, I burned
under its gaze and under the gaze
of a Man who was famished
for my white underskin.
The waves went suddenly quiet

And I was possessed through waterweed
over warm stones, away to a future
woven by flesh not my own.
The same sun swung east to west
over the years weaving
these human strands into a family
that walked on the stones.

It was the youngest, our peedie lass
who asked what was it always
I was looking for. I told her a pretty skin

to make her a shoe. *Bit Mam,*
I ken fine whar hid it is. Wan day
when ye war oot and me Fither

thowt I wis sleepin' he teen a bonnie
skin doon, gloured at hid for cheust
a peedie meenit, then foldit hid
under dae aisins abeun da bed.
I emptied the space where I stood
into the child. Hers to keep.

Dearest, My Little Babar,

Do you remember your professor, the long stringy
       hair, the pince nez?
How he took you straight to Heidegger after your
       times tables?
How the three of us pondered his *Being and Time* like
       a jigsaw puzzle
where we each had a stash of the pieces? Lately I am
       seized by his concept
of truth-seeking as an act of unconcealing. Do you
       remember
as you wolfed down chocolate eclairs and we combed
       through his words
for clear clues to their meaning? Finally, this little Old
       Lady has come near
to the shore where we left those questions.

You were so darling, so large and so lost when we
       met. I knew you were sad
and wanted a suit. Do you remember? And I gave
       you my purse to buy one,
bright green, a shirt and a tie, a derby hat, shoes with
       spats, and an automobile,
shiny and red to ride in each day. I wanted to make
       you my own, dear thing.
You stood on your two hindlegs in my parlor and
       discussed affairs
in your great forest like a well-versed explorer leaning
       into our luxury
with ease. But late at night I heard the shutter shake
       at your window
and knew you were leaning there, weeping there for
       your unbelonging.

It was your tears, how they burned from more than
        mere memory
that were your guide those star-laden nights when you
        shed
the fine clothes, the cane and the spats and stood
        unadorned
in all but your tears. Wonderful tears that kept you
        from being
a changeling under my wing. Woe led you straight to
        your hurt-in-hiding.
Straight home to the headlands of your green jungle
        forest.

You child of my heart,
I've learned all that I know from you.

The Old Lady

Ground Hog

Especially people like me from other countries,
they ask me if we bury people for a few years
then dig them up to make room for somebody else.
I say no, when we bury people it's forever.

In my work you have to be somebody who can
run a machine called a ground hog which is also
an animal that burrows underground like us.
They used to do it by hand with a shovel

but now we just use it to get the ground ready.
Last year we had a frost thirty-five inches deep
that nothing but an air hammer could break through.
My priest he talks about *eternal life* and I know

just what he means. You'd be impressed
to see me digging a grave, how deep, square
perfect I make it. A human body is going there.
When it's my turn, somebody just like me

will ready the earth where I'll be lowered
with the priest's blessing, my kids holding hands.
In less than two minutes they'll open the hoppers,
with the right amount of earth press it down firm

then a layer of sod. When it grows its own roots
it will match the grass around it. Fit in.
When your body's in the grave you own that land.
It's yours forever.

The Trickster

It was a wonder the trees
the trees stayed standing
during such a hot dry summer
in Ohio when my brother and I
got tricked into going back
to a camp we hated
because the director promised
us on Friday before our mother
picked us up to go home
for the weekend that on Monday
he would show us something
that nobody had ever seen
before and that nobody
would see again. Ever.

It turned out to be a peanut.

Come Monday this man
stood on a milk crate
under a tall thirsty sycamore
and held up his promise
cracked its shell —*No one
has ever seen this before*
while chewing the nut
his eyes watered and he stared
at us hard —*And no one will ever
see it again.*

My brother wanted to call home
but there was no phone. He wouldn't
speak to me all that week even when

I hit his arm and pretended
it was a mistake.

Fisherman

Uncle Charlie talked about water
as if it were a book he was reading.
He told us what he saw, no,
what he found, there either
floating by his motorboat
or actually on his fishing line.
A horse's leg, two dead dogs,
a pocketbook full of money,
a sack of kittens, and then
I ran from the room.
The Scioto River became
a story full of riddles.
He tipped his glass and the neck
of the beer bottle together
as if they were talking,
he said they were necking,
and the creamy top rose
and rose to his tongue
waiting against the glass
for the overflow. Too much
time with his dogs Jack and Ebby
taught him to lap up the head
while he smiled his wide smile.
He didn't keep secrets, did not
even try, the way we did.
After my horseshow he wanted
to know why I slumped
the minute the judges appeared
and at swim meets why I dove
deep off the side of the pool.
He said that I swallowed up

luck. He'd learned from watching
I didn't want to win. No other grownup
talked to me like that.

Range-Dusted

Beverly Barker holds the camera,
snaps and that's all that matters.
I sit bareback on my pinto pony,
eleven, reins in one hand,
look at Bev who laughs
and that is why in the photo
I scowl as if a strange
thought surprised me.

It is Bev I am trying to become.
That is each summer's secret.
Even in the cool shaded woods
in the heart of Ohio: to be Bev.
No leaves on the trees so summer
is over. Bev's back from Wyoming.
Her two years' longer legs in Levi's
bought there where she goes every
June to her grandfather's ranch,
swims horseback across rivers,
eats food cooked under stones
in the earth with cowboys,
sleeps under that entire
night sky when she wants.
The photo will prove that my pony's
wide-brush sectioned colors
are watered-down pinto, not western bred.
And Bev, after the click, looks up
and laughing rubs a range-dusted boot
against the back of her leg.

One Problem with Suicide

Truth be told, it's never over.
Wouldn't you think the dead
would want it to be?
After all they meant
to finish the job.
Bullets enter
necks crack
pills congregate
and what a shame
that life goes on anyway
carrying their dead weight
with new specific gravity.
It's enough to make you believe
in life after death.

L.S.M.F.T.

"Lucky Strike Means Fine Tobacco"
introduced on the package in 1945

What was it I wondered as a child
that he took inside of himself,
where did it go? Behind his closed
eyelids was some other place
more exotic than regular breath.

On the day of his death he smoked
a whole pack at his desk.
The crystal ashtray was not big enough
for the crushed shredded ends
that had kept him alive.

My father smoked cigarettes like a man
climbing a ladder, lighting one on
the glowing tip of another. Smoke screened
around him as he pressed a butt
into threads, turning a screw.

What We Call Weather

What we call
weather changes
according to currents
that follow no
scheme except motion.
A cloud has a shape
but just blink
and now only
memory
has hold of that shape.

Before we looked up
there was earth
and all of us
tethered by weight
to her core
we thought was firm.
We cling to form
as different from cloud
because change is explosive
in matter that's dense.

These Earrings

First they were art deco plates and cups from
        a famous hotel
then as things must they shattered from heat
        and collision.
Some hand searched for patterns in each of the pieces
made them smooth and serene in a casing of silver.

As fragile things must they shattered from heat
        and collision.
These earrings were once broken black-and-white crockery
made smooth and serene in a casing of silver
as if the way they became had been someone's intent.

Once broken black-and-white crockery
restored from shards in a bin
as if the way they became was someone's intent
and not surface prepared to survive.

Restored from shards
they became something worn close to the ear
their surface prepared to survive
by the space emptying into us.

Something worn close to the ear—
some hand searched for patterns
to fill the space emptying into us.
But first plates and cups, a famous hotel.

Wild Blue Place
For my mother

I had to practice your absence
after you died and I did, dutifully.
You lay on the gurney so still.
But to check I pulled down
the blanket and prodded your shoulder
first with my finger, then with the flat
of my hand.

By gravetime you disappeared
into a shiny bronze urn
that was nothing like you.
The sky there was wide, sharp,
attentive and as if from that wild
and very blue place
came a soft little gesture
that suited my hand.
It's a rite I still practice dozens
of times every day where my thumb
rubs my forefinger in smooth tiny
circles that say we're each here.